Behind the Scenes
with Coders

WEB DEVELOPER

Melissa Raé Shofner

PowerKiDS
press.

New York

Published in 2018 by The Rosen Publishing Group, Inc.
29 East 21st Street, New York, NY 10010

First Edition

Editor: Melissa Raé Shofner
Book Design: Mickey Harmon
Photo Researcher: Tanya Dellaccio

Photo Credits: Cover, pp. 1, 3–32 (background) Lukas Rs/Shutterstock.com; cover (code) spainter_vfx/Shutterstock.com; cover (man) ESB Professional/Shutterstock.com; p. 5 YanLev/Shutterstock.com; p. 7 racorn/Shutterstock.com; p. 8 PORTRAIT IMAGES ASIA BY NONWARIT/Shutterstock.com; p. 9 Moosey/Shutterstock.com; p. 10 Elnur/Shutterstock.com; p. 13 Ariel Skelley/Blend Images/Getty Images; p. 14 An147yus/Shutterstock.com; pp. 15, 20, 23 Rawpixel.com/Shutterstock.com; pp. 17, 21 dotshock/Shutterstock.com; p. 19 wavebreakmedia/Shutterstock.com; p. 25 xavierarnau/E+/Getty Images; p. 27 goodluz/Shutterstock.com; p. 29 Hero Images/Getty Images.

Cataloging-in-Publication Data

Names: Shofner, Melissa Raé.
Title: Web developer / Melissa Raé Shofner.
Description: New York : PowerKids Press, 2018. | Series: Behind the scenes with coders | Includes index.
Identifiers: ISBN 9781508155737 (pbk.) | ISBN 9781508155676 (library bound) | ISBN 9781508155553 (6 pack)
Subjects: LCSH: Web site development–Juvenile literature. | Web sites–Design–Juvenile literature.
Classification: LCC TK5105.888 S56 2018 | DDC 006.7–dc23

Manufactured in the United States of America

CPSIA Compliance Information: Batch BS17PK: For Further Information contact Rosen Publishing, New York, New York at 1-800-237-9932

Contents

Websites for Everything

Today, people use websites for many things. We pay bills, conduct research, read the news, send e-mails, shop for clothes, play games, and more. We're even able to take college courses and video chat with friends around the world. There are few areas of our lives that don't involve computers and websites in some way.

Even though we use websites all the time, we rarely stop to think about the people who work behind the scenes to create them. These people are called web developers, and their job involves a lot of planning, organizing, and coding. People skills are also very important. If you enjoy working with computers and people and are interested in learning how to code, you may want to consider becoming a web developer.

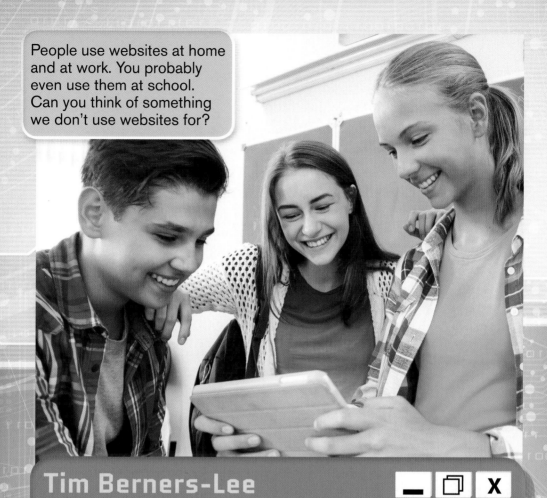

People use websites at home and at work. You probably even use them at school. Can you think of something we don't use websites for?

Tim Berners-Lee ▬ ❐ X

Tim Berners-Lee was born in 1955 and studied physics at Oxford University. In 1980, Berners-Lee first described his idea for a system that would allow researchers around the world to share information with each other. He later developed a similar system and named it the World Wide Web. He also created the first **web browser**. In 1991, he launched the first website, which explained the World Wide Web and told others how to make their own sites.

5

Basic Job Description

What do web developers do? The simple answer is that they build websites. However, they do much more than just that. Web developers are the brains behind the **technical** end of creating a website.

Before they can get down to coding, though, web developers spend time talking to their **clients** about what they expect from their site. Skilled web developers can create websites that fit perfectly with their clients' wants and needs. Website development can take a long time and may involve many people.

A web developer's job doesn't end after a website is built. A site must be tested and updated regularly. This keeps a website looking and working great, which keeps clients and site users happy.

Development Versus Design

Web development and web design aren't the same thing. Designers work on the creative side of a project. They make sure a website looks nice and is user friendly. Developers work on the technical side of a project. They write the code that makes a website work. Designers and developers work together and often know a lot about each other's jobs. This can be very helpful when it comes to creating a great website.

Creating a great website is a lot like creating a great car. Developers build the car and make sure the parts, such as the engine and the brakes, all work properly. Designers make sure the car has comfortable seats and a shiny coat of paint.

Coding Is Key

A large part of a web developer's job is writing the code for a website, but what is code? Code is what tells a computer what to do. Computers only understand very basic "on" and "off" directions from switches called transistors. Transistors turned on and off in different combinations are what make computers do everything they do.

001 00000 1011101 0 11000101 11111000 01111111 11000110 00110111 00111 0

00111101 10111000 11111110 00011011 11010010 11100111 0001 0111 100000

01110011 00000000 10010111 10001110 11110101 10111111 11111111 10001 0

10001110 11101000 00010001 11111000 00000100 01101111 11110100 110111

01111100 10011101 11110101 11101010 10011111 10000010 11000100 001000

11111100 10001110 11000111 10110110 00011001 11111000 11000001 111001

01110111 10001101 01111111 00011110 11010111 00100010 00011100 11101 0

0001 0000 1000110 11011111 10101111 11001111 00111111 11110101 111001

01010110 11111110 00110011 11011111 00011111 00101001 00011111 101111

10000000 00111111 10101110 01111111 000001

10111000 00010001 11111000 01000111 001111

10011000 11000111 11101000 11010111 101011

11100000 11111111 00111110 01111111 10001 0

00001101 11110101 11101110 00110101 00100 1

Binary makes it easier for people to understand the on-off transistor combinations that computers use, but it's still too **complicated** for people to actually write code with.

Today's computers may contain billions of transistors. Binary code represents transistor combinations using 0s and 1s. A combination of eight transistors is represented by a group of eight digits. In binary code, a capital letter "C" is 01000011. "Cat" spelled in binary code would be: 01000011 01100001 01110100. If a simple three-letter word such as "Cat" is represented by so many 1s and 0s, imagine how much binary code is behind your favorite website.

Programming Languages

Everything you see on a website has code behind it that's been written by a web developer—and there's a lot more on a website than just the word "Cat." If it's impossible to write code using on-off transistor combinations or binary, how do web developers do their job? They use programming languages.

Tech Talk ● ● ●

A text file written in a programming language is called a program. The code within a program is called source code. How you run a program depends on what language it's written in. For example, a JavaScript program runs in a web browser.

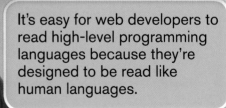

It's easy for web developers to read high-level programming languages because they're designed to be read like human languages.

High-Level and Low-Level Languages

— ◻ X

There are two main types of programming languages. High-level languages use words and symbols that people can understand. They're designed in a way that's easy for us to read and write. Web developers sometimes use high-level languages such as Perl and PHP. Low-level languages, such as assembly and machine languages, are very basic. They're closer to binary and are easier for computers to understand. Sometimes people will code with assembly languages, but machine languages can't be read by humans.

A programming language is a set of **syntax** rules and commands that allow people to communicate with computers. Web developers use these languages to write lines of code, which are instructions for the computer. A special program called a compiler translates these instructions into binary code that a computer can understand.

There are thousands of programming languages. Web developers should know how to use HTML5 and Cascading Style Sheets (CSS). Knowledge of Java, JavaScript, and other programming languages is also useful.

Front-End and Back-End Developers

Websites have a front end and a back end. The front end is everything seen on-screen when a website is displayed in a browser. Front-end developers focus on making user-friendly websites. They make sure users can easily interact with the elements displayed on a site, such as drop-down menus. Front-end developers often use HTML5, CSS, and JavaScript to write code because these programming languages work right in a browser.

Back-end developers focus on the data that's sent from a **web server** to a browser. They handle the working parts of a website that users don't see on their screen. These parts need to work together correctly so there aren't problems on the front end. Back-end developers often write code in languages such as PHP, Python, and Ruby.

Front-end developers work on client-side scripting, which is the code for everything on a website people can see. Back-end developers work on server-side scripting, which is the code that operates behind the scenes to make a website work.

Full-Stack Developers

Front-end and back-end developers need to know a lot of information about their respective parts of a website. They also need to understand how the different ends relate to each other. Front-end developers often have a working knowledge of programming languages used for back-end development and vice versa.

Tech Talk

Some web developers focus on becoming an expert in one programming language. For example, they could become a PHP developer. Instead of dealing with a whole project, they may be hired to build just a certain part of a new website.

```
$pathSegments = explode(
$c = count($pathSegments
$pathToCurrentInnerLink
for($j = 0; $j < $c-1;
        $pathToCurrentInner
return $pathToCurrentIn
```

Today, a client looking for someone to build a website may seek a full-stack developer.

Some web developers, however, work on both the front end and back end of a website. These people are called full-stack developers. Full-stack developers know a lot about both the client side and the server side of web development and can build an entire website all on their own. They get this name because they understand all the programs that are needed for web development. This full group of programs is known as a web stack.

Essential Skills

There are a few essential, or necessary, skills that web developers need to have regardless of what part of a project they're working on. Excellent communication skills are key. This is because one of the main things web developers do besides write code is talk to people. It also helps to be a "people person."

Web development often involves working with a team to create a client's website. Besides the client, web developers need to communicate closely with people such as designers, illustrators, and content writers. No matter who they're talking to, they must be able to communicate their ideas in nontechnical language so everyone understands and is on the same page. This is especially important when talking to a client about what they're hoping to achieve with their new website.

Web development is all about what the client wants. A good web developer will be able to tell a client if their hopes for a site are possible and offer alternatives if they aren't.

Tech Talk ● ● ●

Web developers are sort of like project managers. They need to be able to set goals, meet deadlines, and keep the whole team working toward the same results.

Having a Plan

Since web developers work so closely with clients when building a site, there needs to be transparency, or open sharing of information about a project. Transparency requires honesty, good communication, and accountability. When someone is held accountable, it means they're required to be responsible for their work.

One way to encourage transparency when building a website is to create a detailed plan for each stage of the project. The client and the developer both need to agree on this plan, which is called a web development process.

A web development process lets the client see what's going on with a project during each stage so they know things are on track. Having a solid plan in place makes a developer look professional and builds trust with a client.

A web development process helps a project run smoothly. Everyone will be calmer and more organized, and the workplace will be a more enjoyable space.

Tech Talk

The web development process for each project a developer handles will be different. Each plan will vary depending on what the client wants, the size of the project, the web stack used, and the number of team members.

Building a Website

Web developers first meet with clients to discuss the details of their website. The developer must then decide what **technology**, including programming languages, is right for the project. Every website is different and developers should think carefully about what will work best for each client's needs.

Web developers work hard to make their code perfect. They continue to search for errors and fix code even after a website launches. User **feedback** is very helpful for this.

After creating a web development process, a developer gets to work building a website. They write the code that powers the site. They may also oversee the production of content for the site, although some developers create and edit content themselves. Developers must also convert site content to **formats** that will work on the web.

Before a website is launched, developers search for bugs, which are errors in the code. They debug, or test their code and fix the errors, several times to make sure everything on a site works properly.

Updates and Improvements

A website is never truly finished. Technology is constantly advancing and websites are always in need of updates and improvements. Web developers may eventually need to update a site's content or make changes to its format. Changes in technology also mean a website's security features may need to be updated from time to time.

Web developers analyze, or carefully study, a website's performance over time. They also review feedback from people who use the site. This feedback can be very valuable as it lets the client and developer know what users think of their website. If users find a site hard to use or if parts of a site don't work properly, a client may lose business. Web developers should have patience when dealing with requests for changes from clients.

Web developers may meet with their clients after a website launches to talk about the site's performance, go over user feedback, and discuss possible improvements.

In the Workplace

Web developers have many choices when it comes to deciding where to work. Some work for small companies—often called shops or studios—that create websites for clients. Others work for larger companies as in-house developers. A web developer may also work with a team of experts at a large company within the technology industry.

According to the U.S. Bureau of Labor Statistics, about one in seven web developers were self-employed in 2014. This means they worked for themselves. Self-employed developers sometimes run their own small development businesses. Sometimes they take on freelance work. This is work done for a client without committing to long-term employment with them.

Web developers usually work about 40 hours a week. Some positions offer **flexible** schedules. Sometimes developers may need to work nights or weekends.

People who work as in-house developers for a company may work alone or on a team with other technology experts.

What to Study

There are many things you can do now to prepare yourself for a career in web development. Taking math, science, and computer classes in middle and high school will give you a better idea of your strengths and weaknesses. You'll be able to decide if web development might be a good fit for you. Remember that web developers also need excellent communication skills, so taking English classes will also be helpful.

Many web developers have a degree in computer science or computer programming. Many colleges offer computer-related courses, and there are also special technology colleges. You might want to look at these schools for programs that focus on web development. Keep in mind that many web developers have knowledge of front-end and back-end development, as well as web design.

An internship is a job done, often without pay, in order to gain work experience. Employers and clients look for web developers with real-world experience, so it's a good idea to take an internship if you have the opportunity.

Other Ways to Learn

There are many ways to learn about web development outside the classroom. Some web developers are self-taught. This means they didn't go to college to learn about web development. Instead, they learned by reading books and articles about building websites. Watching videos online is also a great way to learn about coding and web development. There are many websites that offer free instructions on how to work with many popular coding languages.

Of course, one of the best ways to learn is by doing. Practicing coding and building simple websites can be a lot of fun. You may also be able to find an adult who works in the industry who is willing to talk to you about web development. Having a **mentor** is a great way to learn.

You may be able to attend technology conferences in your area. These are great places to learn about the latest advances in coding and web development.

Tech Talk

Professional web developers need to have a love of learning so they can stay on top of advances in technology.

The Future of Web Development

We use technology, including websites, more and more each day. It's not surprising that the web development field continues to grow. The U.S. Bureau of Labor Statistics estimates that the number of developer jobs will increase by about 27 percent through 2024. As of 2015, many web developers in the United States made about $65,000 a year.

Before job hunting, a web developer should build a strong portfolio. A portfolio is a collection of your best web development work. If you're just starting out, you can use work that you did at school or an internship or even on your own. Stay on top of changing technology and continue to practice your coding skills. Everyone wants a website, which makes the future of web development look very promising.

Glossary

client: An individual or company that pays someone else to do something.

complicated: Difficult to explain or understand.

feedback: Information about reactions to something used as a basis for improvement.

flexible: Being able to move and bend in many ways; willing and able to change.

format: A general plan for how something should be organized or arranged.

mentor: A person who teaches and gives guidance or advice to someone else, especially a less experienced person.

syntax: How words are arranged to form a sentence.

technical: Of or relating to a mechanical or scientific subject.

technology: A method that uses science to solve problems and the tools used to solve those problems.

web browser: A computer program that allows users to search the Internet.

web server: A computer or computer program that dispenses web pages as they are requested.

Index

Websites